# Dump

# Dump Dinners Cookbook

## *Simple And Delicious Dump Dinner Recipes For The Whole Family*

# Table Of Contents

# Introduction

This book contains dump dinner recipes for you and your family.

Nowadays, everybody is spending so much more time at work or in school that they have less time to prepare delicious meals at home. However, constantly eating out and resorting to microwaveable meals are unhealthy and unsatisfying. The good news is that there is a solution to this: Dump Dinners.

Dump dinners are dishes that require minimal effort but provide maximum flavor. When preparing a dump dinner, all you have to do is combine a variety of healthy ingredients in one pot and then let your oven or slow cooker do most of the work for you. You will be able to spend more time on other important tasks at home while waiting for your dinner to finish cooking.

In this book, you will first learn how to make your own broths and tomato paste in bulk so that you can minimize the use of canned ingredients. All of the recipes call for affordable and easy-to-find ingredients, so buying your groceries is also hassle-free. Best of all, you have a wide selection of dump dinner recipes, including soups and stews; pizzas and pastas; vegetable, beef, pork, poultry and seafood dishes; and even dump cake recipes for desserts!

Let's begin the journey.

# Chapter 1: Healthy Homemade Basics

## Chicken Broth

Makes: 9 cups

*What You'll Need:*

3 quarts cold water

6 pounds chicken pieces (such as neck, back, wings, bones, and/or legs)

3 onions or 2 leeks, chopped

3 celery stalks, chopped

2 carrots, chopped

12 black peppercorns

3 sprigs fresh parsley

3 sprigs fresh thyme

1 1/2 teaspoon sea salt

*How to Prepare:*

Pour the cold water into the stock pot, then add the chicken pieces.

Place over high flame and bring to a boil, skimming the foam off the surface.

3. Add the onions or leeks, celery, carrots, black peppercorns, parsley, thyme, and salt. Stir to combine, and then bring to a boil.

4. Reduce to a simmer and cook, uncovered, for 2 hours.

5. Remove from the flame and set aside to cool to room temperature. Strain the soup, discarding the solids.

6. Chill the soup, then skim off the solidified fat that forms on the surface. Divide into separate containers and refrigerate for 2 to 3 weeks or freeze for up to 3 months.

# Beef Broth

Number of Servings: 9 cups

*What You'll Need:*

- Olive oil

  6 pounds beef or veal bones

  1 1/2 pounds stew meat (such as flank or chuck steak), chopped

  3 onions, peeled and quartered

- 3 large carrots, chopped

  3 quarts cold water

  2 celery ribs, chopped

- 5 garlic cloves, unpeeled

  12 sprigs fresh thyme

  12 sprigs fresh parsley

  3 bay leaves

  15 black peppercorns

*How to Prepare:*

Set the oven to 375 degrees Fahrenheit to preheat. Coat the stew meat, onions, and carrots with olive oil, and then arrange the pieces along with the bones on a roasting pan.

Roast for 50 minutes, turning the pieces within the first 30 minutes of cooking time.

3.  Transfer the roasted ingredients into a large pot along with th
    juices collected in the roasting pan.

4.  Add the bay leaves, celery, parsley, black peppercorns, a
    garlic to the mixture, then fill with enough cold water t
    submerge all of the ingredients by 1 inch.

5.  Place over medium-high flame and bring to a simmer, an
    then reduce heat to lowest possible setting. Partially cover an
    cook for 4 hours.

6.  Remove the pot from the flame and set aside to cool to roo
    temperature. Skim the fat from the surface, and then strain t
    soup and discard the solids.

7.  Divide into separate containers and refrigerate for up to
    weeks or freeze for up to 3 months.

## Vegetable Broth

Makes: 9 cups

*What You'll Need:*

- 1 1/2 tablespoons coconut oil
- 2 medium onions, chopped
- 3 celery stalks with leaves, chopped
- 3 large carrots, peeled and chopped
- 2 bunches green onion, chopped
- 1 garlic bulb, peeled and minced
- 12 sprigs fresh thyme
- 12 sprigs fresh parsley
- 3 bay leaves
- 1 1/2 teaspoon sea salt
- 3 quarts water

*How to Prepare:*

Place a large stock pot over medium heat and heat the coconut oil. Stir in the onions, carrot, celery, garlic, green onions, bay leaves, thyme, and parsley. Sauté for 7 minutes.

Pour in the water and add the salt. Stir and bring to a boil, and then reduce to a simmer and cook, uncovered, for half an hour.

3.  Strain the soup, discarding the solids. Let stand to cool t
    room temperature, and then divide into separate container
    and refrigerate for up to 3 weeks or freeze for up to 3 months.

## Tomato Paste

Makes: 9 cups

*What You'll Need:*

- 7 1/2 pounds plum tomatoes, chopped
- 1/2 cup olive oil
- Sea salt

*How to Prepare:*

Place a skillet over medium heat and heat the olive oil. Add the plum tomatoes and season with salt.

Increase heat and bring to a boil. Cook until tomatoes become extremely soft, stirring occasionally.

Pour the mixture into the food mill with the finest plate attached, pressing down on the pulp to extract as much out of it as possible. Collect in a skillet.

Place the skillet over medium-high flame, and then bring to a boil. Reduce to a simmer, and let simmer for 1 hour or until thickened to a paste.

Set aside to cool to room temperature. Then, pour into sterilized glass jars, seal, and refrigerate for up to 1 month. Alternatively, store in airtight containers and freeze for up to 6 months.

# Chapter 2: Soup and Stew Recipes

**Chicken Enchilada Soup**

Number of Servings: 9

*What You'll Need:*

➢ 1 small onion, peeled and chopped

➢ 1 1/2 tablespoon garlic, minced

➢ 5 1/4 cups chicken broth

➢ 12 ounces tomato sauce

➢ 21 ounces canned pinto beans, rinsed and drained

➢ 21 ounces tomatoes, diced

➢ 21 ounces canned corn kernels

➢ 1 1/2 teaspoon ground cumin

➢ 3/4 teaspoon dried oregano

➢ 2 1/2 pounds skinless and boneless chicken breasts, cube and partially cooked

➢ 3/4 cup cheddar cheese, finely grated

➢ 3 tablespoons green onion, minced

➢ 1 1/2 tablespoons fresh cilantro, chopped

➢ 1 large avocado, peeled, seeded, and diced

➢ Optional: sour cream and crushed tortilla chips

*How to Prepare:*

- Combine the onions, garlic, broth, tomato sauce, pinto beans, tomatoes, corn kernels, cumin, oregano, and chicken breast in a slow cooker.

- Cover and cook for 5 hours on low heat.

- Ladle into soup bowls and top with cheddar cheese, green onion, cilantro, avocado, and sour cream with crushed tortilla chips, if desired.

- To store, allow to cool to room temperature, and then transfer into airtight containers and freeze.

## Vegetable Stew

Number of Servings: 3

*What You'll Need:*

- ➢ 3 cups carrots, sliced
- ➢ 1 1/2 cups celery, finely sliced stalks
- ➢ 1 1/2 cups mushrooms, finely sliced
- ➢ 3 cups vegetable broth
- ➢ 1 1/2 cups red bell peppers, sliced
- ➢ 1 white onion, sliced
- ➢ 2 cups tomatoes, chopped
- ➢ Sea salt
- ➢ Freshly ground black pepper

*How to Prepare:*

1. Set the oven to 400 degrees Fahrenheit to preheat.

2. In an oven-safe pot, pour in the carrots, celery, mushrooms, bell pepper, onion, and tomatoes. Add the broth, and then stir and season to taste with salt and pepper.

3. Place the pot in the oven (make sure it's covered) and cook to 60 minutes. Carefully take out of the oven and serve at once.

## Sausage and Tortellini Soup

Number of Servings: 6

*What You'll Need:*

- 2 1/2 cups beef broth
- 2 cups French onion soup
- 2 1/2 cups tomatoes, chopped
- 2 pounds Italian sausage, cooked, drained, and sliced
- 1 1/2 tablespoons fresh basil, chopped
- 4 1/2 cups water
- 2 cups cheese tortellini, frozen

*How to Prepare:*

1. Combine the beef broth, water, and onion soup in the slow cooker.

2. Stir in the tomatoes, sausage, basil, and tortellini.

   Cover and cook for 8 hours on low heat. Serve warm.

## Squash and Chickpea Stew

Number of Servings: 4

*What You'll Need:*

➢ 1 1/2 pounds butternut squash, diced

➢ 3 cups carrots, sliced

➢ 1 1/2 cups canned chickpeas, drained

➢ 1 1/2 cups celery, finely sliced

➢ 1 white onion, sliced

➢ 3/4 cup tomato paste

➢ 5 cups vegetable broth

➢ 3/4 cup fresh chives, chopped

➢ 1/3 cup fresh parsley, chopped

➢ Sea salt

➢ Freshly ground black pepper

*How to Prepare:*

1. Set the oven to 400 degrees Fahrenheit to preheat.

2. Combine the squash, carrots, chickpeas, celery, onion, tomato paste, and broth in an oven-safe pot. Stir in the chives and parsley, and then season with salt and pepper.

3. Place the pot in the oven (make sure it's covered) and cook for 60 minutes. Carefully take out of the oven and serve at once.

## Beef and Split Pea Stew

Number of Servings: 6

*What You'll Need:*

- 1 1/2 pounds beef stew meat, cubed
- 2 leeks, chopped
- 1 small onion, chopped
- 2 bay leaves
- 4 cups chicken broth
- 3/4 cup green split peas
- 1/3 cup yellow split peas
- 3 tablespoons golden raisins
- 1 1/2 tablespoons lemon juice
- 1 teaspoon ground cumin
- 3/4 teaspoon dried oregano
- 1/3 teaspoon garlic salt
- 1/3 teaspoon freshly ground black pepper

*How to Prepare:*

Combine the beef, onion, leeks, split peas, and oregano in the slow cooker.

Pour in the broth, and then add the bay leaves, lemon juice, cumin, salt, and pepper. Stir once.

3. Cover and cook for 7 hours on low heat.

4. Remove the bay leaves and serve warm.

# Easy Beef Stew

Number of Servings: 6

## What You'll Need:

- 2 pounds beef stew meat, chopped into chunks
- 2 cups canned tomato soup
- 5 carrots, peeled and sliced
- 5 potatoes, peeled and cubed
- 6 celery stalks, cleaned and sliced
- 2 onions, peeled and chopped
- 1 1/2 teaspoons brown sugar
- 3 tablespoons dry tapioca
- 1 1/2 cups water

## How to Prepare:

1. In a slow cooker, combine the tomato soup, brown sugar, water, and tapioca.

2. Add the beef, carrots, potatoes, celery, and onion. Stir to combine.

3. Cover and cook for 8 hours on low heat, or for 4 hours on high heat. Serve warm.

## Cauliflower Stew

Number of Servings: 6

*What You'll Need:*

- ➢ 4 cups cauliflower florets
- ➢ 2 fennels, sliced
- ➢ 2 eggplants, sliced
- ➢ 3 carrots, sliced
- ➢ 1 1/2 cups celery, chopped
- ➢ 2 small onions, sliced
- ➢ 3 cups vegetable broth
- ➢ 3 tablespoons olive oil
- ➢ 1/2 cup fresh flat leaf parsley, chopped
- ➢ Sea salt
- ➢ Freshly ground black pepper

*How to Prepare:*

1. Set the oven to 400 degrees Fahrenheit to preheat.

2. In an oven-safe pot, combine the cauliflower florets, fennel, eggplants, carrots, celery, onions, parsley and vegetable broth. Drizzle the olive oil over the mixture, and then season with salt and pepper.

3. Place the pot into the oven and cook for 60 minutes. Carefully take out of the oven and serve at once.

# Lentil Stew

Number of Servings: 4

*What You'll Need:*

- 1 cup dry lentils
- 3 cups chicken broth
- 3 tomatoes, seeded and chopped
- 1 small potato, chopped
- 1 small carrot, peeled and chopped
- 1 small onion, chopped
- 1/2 cup celery, chopped
- 3 sprigs fresh flat leaf parsley
- 1 garlic clove, minced
- 1 pound lean pork or beef, cubed
- Freshly ground black pepper

*How to Prepare:*

In a soup pot, combine the lentils, broth, meat, tomato, potato, carrot, onion, celery, parsley, and garlic. Season with black pepper.

Cover and cook over medium heat for 35 minutes, or until the meat is cooked through. Serve at once.

## Roasted Bell Pepper Soup

Number of Servings: 6

*What You'll Need:*

- ➢ 24 oz roasted red bell peppers in jars, drained
- ➢ 2 large carrots, peeled and chopped
- ➢ 3 1/2 cups vegetable broth
- ➢ 3/4 cup white wine or additional broth
- ➢ 1/2 teaspoon garlic salt
- ➢ 1/2 teaspoon paprika
- ➢ 1/4 teaspoon freshly ground black pepper
- ➢ 1 1/2 tablespoons Parmesan cheese, freshly grated
- ➢ Fresh chives, chopped

*How to Prepare:*

1. Coat the inside of the slow cooker with nonstick cooking spray.
2. Dump the bell peppers, carrots, paprika, black pepper, and garlic salt in the slow cooker.
3. Pour in the vegetable broth and wine. Stir once.
4. Cover and cook for 5 hours on low heat. If preferred, blend the soup afterward.
5. Before serving, add the cheese. Cover and cook for 10 minutes on high or until melted.
6. Sprinkle fresh chives on top and serve.

# Healthy Hungarian Pea Stew

Number of Servings: 6

*What You'll Need:*

- 4 cups green peas
- 3/4 pound boneless lean pork, cubed
- 1 1/2 tablespoons olive oil
- 3 tablespoons almond flour
- 1 1/2 tablespoons fresh flat leaf parsley, chopped
- 3/4 cup water
- 1/3 teaspoon sea salt
- 3/4 cup coconut milk
- 3/4 teaspoon coconut sugar

*How to Prepare:*

Combine the olive oil, green peas, and pork cubes in a pot over medium heat and simmer for 10 minutes, or until tender.

Stir in the coconut sugar, almond flour, chopped parsley, and salt. Let simmer for 1 minute.

Stir in the coconut milk and water. Cover and cook for 4 minutes over low heat. Serve at once.

## Dump Dinner Ratatouille

Number of Servings: 6

*What You'll Need:*

- ➢ 3 potatoes, cubed
- ➢ 5 medium-sized tomatoes, seeded and chopped
- ➢ 3 eggplants, cubed
- ➢ 5 zucchinis, cubed
- ➢ 3 red bell peppers, seeded and sliced
- ➢ 3 red onions, chopped
- ➢ 3 garlic cloves, minced
- ➢ 3 cups mushrooms, finely sliced
- ➢ 3 tablespoons olive oil
- ➢ 1 1/2 tablespoons red wine vinegar
- ➢ 1/3 cup white wine
- ➢ 3/4 teaspoon dried thyme
- ➢ 3/4 teaspoon dried oregano
- ➢ 1/3 cup fresh flat leaf parsley, chopped
- ➢ Sea salt
- ➢ Freshly ground black pepper

*How to Prepare:*

Set the oven to 400 degrees Fahrenheit to preheat.

In an oven-safe pot, combine the vinegar, olive oil, white wine, thyme, oregano, and parsley.

Add the potatoes, tomatoes, eggplants, zucchinis, red bell peppers, onions, garlic, and mushrooms. Turn to coat in the liquids, and then season with salt and pepper.

Place the pot into oven and cook for 30 minutes, or until the vegetables are all tender. Carefully take out of the oven and serve at once.

## Vegetable and Lamb Stew

Number of Servings: 4

*What You'll Need:*

➢ 1 pound lamb stew meat

➢ 1 large tomato, chopped

➢ 1 small summer squash, cubed

➢ 1 zucchini, cubed

➢ 1/2 cup mushrooms, finely sliced

➢ 1/4 cup bell peppers, chopped

➢ 1/2 cup onions, chopped

➢ 1 teaspoon sea salt

➢ 1 garlic clove, crushed

➢ 1/4 teaspoon dried thyme

➢ 1 bay leaf

➢ 1 cup chicken broth

*How to Prepare:*

1. Combine the lamb stew meat, tomato, squash, zucchi... mushrooms, bell peppers, onion, garlic, thyme, and bay leaf the slow cooker.

2. Season with salt and pour the broth over the mixture.

3. Cover and cook for 7 hours on low heat. Serve warm preferably with rice.

# Chapter 3: Pizza and Pasta Recipes

## Gluten-Free Salami Pizza

Number of Servings: 6

*What You'll Need:*

- 1 1/2 cups full fat cream cheese
- 3 eggs
- 3 tablespoons Parmesan cheese, grated
- 1 1/2 teaspoons garlic powder
- 3/4 cup pizza sauce
- 3 cups mozzarella cheese, finely grated
- 1 cup pepperoni, sliced
- 1 cup salami, sliced
- 9 button mushrooms, sliced
- 2 bell peppers, seeded and sliced thinly
- Garlic powder

*How to Prepare:*

1. Set the oven to 350 degrees Fahrenheit to preheat. Coat a baking sheet with nonstick cooking spray or line with parchment paper.

2. Using an electric mixer, combine the cream cheese, eggs, garlic powder, and Parmesan cheese. Pour the mixture on the prepared baking sheet.

3. Bake for 12 minutes or until golden brown.

4. Remove the crust from the oven and set on a wire rack to cool for 12 minutes.

5. Pour the pizza sauce on top, and then sprinkle with mozzarella cheese. Arrange the toppings and season with garlic powder.

6. Bake for 10 minutes or until cheese melts. Set on a wire rack cool for 5 minutes. Slice and serve.

# Chicago Deep-Dish Pizza

Number of Servings: 9

*What You'll Need:*

- 3 tablespoons olive oil
- 1 1/2 pounds hot Italian pork sausage, casings removed
- 1 1/2 cups onions, minced
- 1 1/2 teaspoon red pepper flakes
- 2/3 cup green bell pepper, chopped
- 12 ounces button mushrooms, sliced
- 5 garlic cloves, minced
- 1 1/2 tablespoons tomato paste
- 24 ounces canned tomato sauce
- 1 1/2 teaspoons dried oregano
- 3/4 teaspoon fennel seeds, crushed
- 15 ounces canned refrigerated pizza crust dough
- 9 slices fresh mozzarella cheese
- 1 1/2 cups mozzarella cheese, finely grated
- 1 1/2 cups Parmesan cheese, grated

*How to Prepare:*

1. Set the oven to 400 degrees Fahrenheit to preheat. Ligh grease an 11 x 14 inch casserole dish with nonstick cooki spray.

2. Cook the sausage in a skillet until brown and crumbled. Dr and set aside.

3. Unroll the pizza crust dough in the casserole dish and pr down to secure. Arrange the sliced mozzarella on top, follow by the sausage.

4. Scatter the onions, bell peppers, mushrooms, and garlic top.

5. Season with the red pepper flakes, oregano, and fennel seed

6. Combine the tomato paste and tomato sauce in a bowl, a... then pour all over the uncooked pizza.

7. Top with finely grated mozzarella and grated Parmesan. B for 25 minutes or until cheese melts and crust is golden bro Set on a wire rack to cool for 10 minutes. Serve.

# Hawaiian Pizza

Number of Servings: 6

*What You'll Need:*

- 1 1/2 cups full fat cream cheese
- 3 eggs
- 3 tablespoons Parmesan cheese, grated
- 1 1/2 teaspoons garlic powder
- 3/4 cup pizza sauce
- 3 cups mozzarella cheese, finely grated
- 3 cups pineapple tidbits, drained
- 2 cups ham, glazed and chopped
- 9 button mushrooms, sliced
- Garlic powder

*How to Prepare:*

1. Set the oven to 350 degrees Fahrenheit to preheat. Coat a baking sheet with nonstick cooking spray or line with parchment paper.

2. Using an electric mixer, combine the cream cheese, eggs, garlic powder, and Parmesan cheese. Pour the mixture on the prepared baking sheet.

3. Bake for 12 minutes or until golden brown.

4. Remove the crust from the oven and set on a wire rack to cool for 12 minutes.

5. Pour the pizza sauce on top, and then sprinkle with mozzarella cheese. Arrange the toppings and season with garlic powder.

6. Bake for 10 minutes or until cheese melts. Set on a wire rack cool for 5 minutes. Slice and serve.

## Tuna Noodle Casserole

Number of Servings: 5

*What You'll Need:*

- 8 ounces button mushrooms, sliced
- 1 1/2 cups bread crumbs, seasoned and toasted in butter
- 1 small onion, chopped
- 2 1/2 cups chicken broth
- 2/3 cup heavy cream
- 6 ounces wide egg noodles
- 4 ounces white tuna in can, packed in water, drained thoroughly, and flaked
- 3/4 cup frozen peas
- 1 1/2 cups Parmesan cheese, grated
- 1 1/2 tablespoons fresh flat leaf parsley leaves, minced
- 3/4 teaspoon paprika
- Cayenne pepper
- Sea salt
- Freshly ground black pepper

*How to Prepare:*

1. Set the oven to 475 degrees Fahrenheit to preheat.

2. Sauté the onion and mushrooms and season with paprika cayenne, and salt until browned. Add the heavy cream ar broth, and then the noodles. Set heat to high and cook un noodles are almost tender.

3. Turn off the heat and add the tuna, peas, parsley, ar Parmesan cheese. Season with salt and pepper.

4. Pour the mixture into a 9 x 13 inch casserole dish and top wi the bread crumbs.

5. Bake for 8 minutes. Serve.

## ot Mac 'n' Cheese

umber of Servings: 6

*hat You'll Need:*

  2 cups fresh broccoli florets, blanched

  1 1/4 cups elbow macaroni, cooked

  1/3 cup sun-dried tomatoes (soaked in warm water for 10 minutes), chopped

  1 1/2 tablespoons unsalted butter

  4 tablespoons green onions, sliced

  1 1/2 tablespoons all-purpose flour

  1 1/2 teaspoon cayenne

  1 teaspoon dried basil

  3/4 teaspoon sea salt

  1 1/3 cups whole milk

  1 cup Cheddar cheese, finely grated

  3/4 cup Gruyere cheese, grated

  3/4 cup Gouda cheese, grated

*w to Prepare:*

Set the oven to 350 degrees Fahrenheit to preheat.

Combine the flour, cayenne, basil, and salt.

3. Sauté the green onions in a skillet with the butter, and then stir in the milk and flour mixture. Stir in the cheeses until melted.

4. Combine the macaroni and broccoli in a 9 x 13 inch casserole dish, and then pour the sauce on top.

5. Bake for 30 minutes, and then set on a wire rack to cool for minutes. Serve warm.

## Four-Cheese Pasta

Number of Servings: 6

*What You'll Need:*

- 14 ounces ziti or other tube pasta, cooked
- 12 ounces canned tomatoes, diced
- 2 tablespoons olive oil
- 3/4 cup onion, chopped
- 9 garlic cloves, minced
- 1/2 cup dry white wine
- 1 1/2 cups heavy cream
- 3/4 cup Gorgonzola cheese, crumbled
- 1 cup Parmesan cheese, finely grated
- 1 1/2 cups mozzarella cheese
- 3/4 cup Fontina cheese, finely grated
- 3/4 teaspoon sea salt
- 2/3 teaspoon freshly ground black pepper

*How to Prepare:*

1. Set the oven to 425 degrees Fahrenheit to preheat. Lightly grease an 8 x 8 inch casserole dish with nonstick cooking spray.

2. Pour the cooked pasta into the casserole, then add the tomatoes with their juices.

3. Sauté the onion and garlic until tender, then add the wine an[d] cook until wine is reduced by half. Stir in the cream and l[et] simmer, and then stir in the Parmesan, Gorgonzol[a], mozzarella, and Fontina.

4. Season to taste with salt and pepper, then pour into th[e] casserole.

5. Bake for 25 to 30 minutes, or until bubbly. Take out of th[e] oven, stir, and place on a wire rack for 5 minutes befo[re] serving.

# Baked Spaghetti

Number of Servings: 8

*What You'll Need:*

- 14 ounces angel hair pasta, cooked
- 1 1/4 tablespoons unsalted butter
- 3/4 cup celery, chopped
- 3/4 cup onion, minced
- 24 ounces canned tomatoes, diced
- 3 ounces canned button mushrooms, sliced
- 2 ounces canned black olives, drained and sliced
- 1 1/2 teaspoons dried oregano
- 1 1/2 cups cheddar cheese, finely grated
- 8 ounces canned cream of mushroom soup
- 4 tablespoons whole milk
- Parmesan cheese, grated

*How to Prepare:*

Set the oven to 350 degrees Fahrenheit to preheat. Lightly grease an 8 x 8 inch casserole dish with nonstick cooking spray.

Melt the butter in a saucepan and sauté the onion and celery, then the tomatoes, mushrooms, olives, and oregano. Let simmer for 8 minutes.

3. Layer half of the cooked pasta in the casserole dish, followed by half the cheddar. Repeat with the second layer. Pour the tomato mixture on top.

4. Combine the milk and cream of mushroom soup and pour over the pasta mixture. Top with Parmesan.

5. Bake for 30 minutes, or until bubbling. Serve warm.

## ~ked Ziti

*hat You'll Need:*

- 2 teaspoons olive oil

- 18 ounces dried ziti, cooked

- 19 ounces hot Italian turkey sausage, with the casings removed

- 6 cups zucchini, thinly sliced

- 2 1/2 cups onions, sliced

- 4 garlic cloves, minced

- 2/3 teaspoon sea salt

- 1/3 teaspoon freshly ground black pepper

- 1/3 teaspoon red pepper flakes

- 3/4 cup chicken broth

- 1/3 cup dry white wine

- 1 1/2 tablespoons all-purpose flour

- 3/4 cup feta cheese, crumbled

- 3/4 cup mozzarella cheese, finely grated

*~w to Prepare:*

Set the oven to 350 degrees Fahrenheit to preheat. Lightly grease a 9 x 13 inch casserole dish with nonstick cooking spray.

2. Brown and crumble the sausage in a pan, then drain the excess grease. Set aside.

3. Sauté the zucchini, onions, and garlic using the olive oil in skillet over medium heat.

4. Whisk the wine, flour, and broth in a bowl, then pour into the zucchini mixture. Bring to a simmer.

5. Combine the feta, sausage, and pasta in the casserole dish then pour the sauce on top. Top with mozzarella cheese.

6. Bake for 20 minutes or until bubbly. Set aside for 10 minutes then serve.

# Chapter 4: Vegetable Recipes

## Chili Red Beans

Number of Servings: 4

*What You'll Need:*

- 4 cups canned red beans, drained
- 2 cups tomatoes, chopped
- 1/2 cup chipotle chilies, diced
- 2 white onions, diced
- 2 green bell peppers, diced
- 1 teaspoon red chili flakes
- 2 teaspoons sweet red paprika
- Sea salt
- Freshly ground black pepper

*How to Prepare:*

Set the oven to 400 degrees Fahrenheit to preheat.

In an oven-safe pot, combine the red beans, tomatoes, chilies, onions, bell peppers, chili flakes, and paprika. Season with salt and pepper to taste.

Place the pot in the oven (make sure it's covered) and cook for 40 minutes. Carefully take out of the oven and serve at once.

## Squash, Eggplant, and Tomato Casserole

Number of Servings: 6

*What You'll Need:*

➢ 5 large tomatoes, sliced

➢ 2 butternut squashes, sliced

➢ 3 large eggplants, sliced

➢ 3 tablespoons olive oil

➢ 2 tablespoons balsamic vinegar

➢ 3 tablespoons Parmesan cheese

➢ 1 1/2 tablespoons fresh flat leaf parsley, chopped

➢ Sea salt

➢ Freshly ground black pepper

*How to Prepare:*

1. Set the oven to 400 degrees Fahrenheit to preheat.

2. In an oven-safe pot, combine the squash, tomato, and eggplant. Season with salt and pepper.

3. Drizzle the balsamic vinegar and olive oil over the mixture then top with parsley and cheese.

4. Place the pot in the oven (make sure it's covered) and cook for 60 minutes. Carefully take out of the oven and serve at once.

## Brown Rice and Peppers

Number of Servings: 6

*What You'll Need:*

- 6 red bell peppers, seeded and sliced
- 3 cups brown rice, uncooked
- 6 cups vegetable broth
- 2 cups carrots, diced
- 2 small onions, diced
- 4 garlic cloves, sliced
- 2 tablespoons fresh parsley, chopped
- Sea salt
- Freshly ground black pepper

*How to Prepare:*

1. Set the oven to 400 degrees Fahrenheit to preheat.

2. In an oven-safe pot, combine the rice and broth, then stir in the bell peppers, carrots, onions, garlic, and fresh parsley. Season with salt and pepper.

3. Place the pot in the oven (make sure it's covered) and cook for 25 minutes. Carefully take out of the oven and serve at once.

# Cauliflower and Yogurt Bake

Number of Servings: 4

*What You'll Need:*

- 4 cups cauliflower florets
- 2 cups Greek yogurt
- 2 cups frozen green beans, thawed and drained
- 2 teaspoons cumin
- 1 teaspoon red chili flakes
- 4 tablespoons olive oil
- Sea salt
- Freshly ground black pepper

*How to Prepare:*

1. Set the oven to 400 degrees Fahrenheit to preheat.

2. In an oven-safe pot, combine the cauliflower and green beans. Drizzle the olive oil over the mixture, then sprinkle the cumin and red chili flakes. Season with salt and pepper to taste, then toss to coat.

3. Place the pot in the oven (make sure it's covered) and bake for 20 minutes. Carefully take out of the oven, stir in the yogurt and serve at once.

## illed Roasted Potatoes

Number of Servings: 5

*What You'll Need:*

- 5 large white potatoes, cubed

- 2 small zucchinis, cubed

- 3 carrots, sliced

- 3/4 cup pine seeds

- 1 1/2 tablespoons olive oil

- 1 1/2 cups water

- 1 1/2 teaspoons fresh dill, chopped

- 1 1/2 teaspoons sweet red paprika

- Sea salt

- Freshly ground black pepper

*How to Prepare:*

Set the oven to 400 degrees Fahrenheit to preheat.

In an oven-safe pot, combine the potatoes, zucchinis, carrots, water, and olive oil. Season with fresh dill, paprika, salt, and pepper. Sprinkle the pine seeds on top.

Place the pot in oven and cook for 60 minutes, or until potatoes are cooked through. Carefully take out of the oven and serve at once.

## Mushroom Casserole

Number of Servings: 6

*What You'll Need:*

- ➤ 4 pounds shiitake mushrooms, sliced
- ➤ 3/4 pound leeks, sliced
- ➤ 3/4 tablespoons fresh flat leaf parsley, chopped
- ➤ 1 large egg, beaten
- ➤ 3/4 cup low-fat Greek yogurt
- ➤ 1/3 cup low-fat cheddar cheese, finely grated
- ➤ 1 pound tofu, cubed
- ➤ Sea salt
- ➤ Freshly ground black pepper

*How to Prepare:*

1. Set the oven to 375 degrees Fahrenheit to preheat.
2. Combine the yogurt and eggs in a bowl.
3. Pour the mushrooms into a casserole, followed by the leek and then the cubed tofu.
4. Season with salt and pepper, then top with parsley. Pour of the yogurt mixture into the casserole, then sprinkle wi half the cheese. Repeat with the second layer.
5. Bake for 15 minutes, or until top is golden brown and chees melted.

## Barley Risotto

Number of Servings: 8

*What You'll Need:*

4 cups barley, uncooked

6 cups water

3/4 cup canned green peas, drained

3/4 cup canned sweet corn, drained

1 large eggplant, sliced

1 large red onion, sliced

Sea salt

Freshly ground black pepper

*How to Prepare:*

Set the oven to 400 degrees Fahrenheit to preheat.

In an oven-safe pot, combine the barley and water. Stir in the sweet corn, green peas, red onion, and eggplant. Season with salt and pepper.

Place the pot in the oven and cook for 45 minutes, or until the barley is fluffy. Carefully take out of the oven and serve at once.

## Turkish Eggplant

Number of Servings: 4

*What You'll Need:*

- ➢ 1 cup couscous
- ➢ 1 cup water
- ➢ 8 garlic cloves, minced
- ➢ 1/2 medium-sized onion, chopped
- ➢ 2 medium-sized eggplants, cubed
- ➢ 15 ounces canned chickpeas, drained and rinsed
- ➢ 1 red bell pepper, seeded and chopped
- ➢ 1 large zucchini, quartered and chopped
- ➢ 30 ounces canned tomatoes, drained and diced
- ➢ 8 shiitake mushrooms, quartered
- ➢ 4 tablespoons fresh marjoram, chopped
- ➢ 4 tablespoons fresh flat leaf parsley, chopped
- ➢ 4 tablespoons sesame seeds
- ➢ 4 teaspoons paprika
- ➢ 1/4 teaspoon red pepper flakes
- ➢ Sea salt
- ➢ Freshly ground black pepper

*How to Prepare:*

Set the oven to 450 degrees Fahrenheit to preheat. Coat an oven-proof baking dish with olive oil.

Pour the couscous and water into the dish, then add the garlic and onion. Add the eggplant, chickpeas, bell pepper, zucchini, tomatoes, and shiitake mushrooms.

Season with salt and pepper.

Add the marjoram, sesame seeds, parsley, red pepper flakes, and paprika.

Cover the dish and bake for 50 minutes, turning the dish once halfway through the cooking time. Serve at once.

## Mushroom and Spinach Casserole

Number of Servings: 6

*What You'll Need:*

➢ 6 cups baby spinach (fresh or frozen), thawed and squeeze dry

➢ 4 cups mushrooms, finely sliced

➢ 2 cups water

➢ 4 garlic cloves, sliced

➢ 2 small onions, sliced

➢ 2 tablespoons olive oil

➢ Sea salt

➢ Freshly ground black pepper

*How to Prepare:*

1. Set the oven to 400 degrees F to preheat.

2. In an oven-safe pot, combine the baby spinach, mushroom, water, garlic, onion, and olive oil. Season with salt and pepper.

3. Place the pot in oven and cook for 30 minutes. Carefully take out of the oven and serve at once.

## Vegetable Curry

Number of Servings: 4

*What You'll Need:*

- 4 garlic cloves, chopped
- 1/2 medium-sized onion, sliced
- 2 fresh jalapeño chilies, stemmed, seeded, and chopped
- 2 cups basmati rice, rinsed well
- 2 cups vegetable broth
- 1 teaspoon ground cumin
- 1 teaspoon ground turmeric
- 1 teaspoon garam masala
- 4 carrots, sliced
- 2 parsnips, sliced
- 4 cups cauliflower florets
- 2 medium-sized zucchini, halved and sliced
- 4 cups green peas, fresh or frozen

*How to Prepare:*

Set the oven to 450 degrees Fahrenheit. Coat a baking dish with nonstick cooking spray.

Place the garlic, onion, and chilies into the dish, then add the rice, broth, garam masala, cumin, and turmeric. Stir to combine.

3. Add the carrots, parsnip, cauliflower, zucchini, and peas.

4. Cover the dish and bake for 50 minutes. Serve at once.

# Chapter 5: Beef Recipes

## Braised Beef with Green Peas

Number of Servings: 2

*What You'll Need:*

- 3 onions, minced
- 3 garlic cloves, chopped
- 1-inch fresh ginger root, peeled and chopped
- 3/4 teaspoon red pepper flakes
- 2 tomatoes, seeded and chopped
- 3 carrots, chopped
- 3 tablespoons coconut oil
- 2 cups beef or chicken broth
- 2 pounds boneless beef, cubed
- 4 cups green peas (fresh or frozen), thawed, and drained
- Sea salt
- Freshly ground black pepper

*How to Prepare:*

Place a heavy saucepan over medium flame and heat the coconut oil. Add the beef, carrots, tomatoes, garlic, onions, ginger, and broth.

2. Cover and let simmer for 40 minutes or until beef is cooked through and most of the liquids have evaporated.

3. Add the green peas and season to taste with red pepper flakes, salt, and pepper. Cover and let simmer until peas are fork tender. Serve at once.

# Slow Cooked Beef Barbecue

Number of Servings: 6

*What You'll Need:*

- 1 cup tomato paste

- 2 1/2 tablespoons lemon juice

- 1 1/2 tablespoons Dijon mustard

- 1/3 teaspoon sea salt

- 1/3 teaspoon freshly ground black pepper

- 3 pounds boneless chuck roast

- 1/3 teaspoon garlic, minced

*How to Prepare:*

Put the chuck roast in a slow cooker and pour the tomato paste, lemon juice, mustard, garlic, salt, and pepper over it. Turn to coat.

Cover and cook for 8 hours on low heat. Serve warm.

## Beef and Special Mushroom Sauce

Number of Servings: 4

*What You'll Need:*

➢  1 medium-sized onion, sliced thinly

➢  2/3 cup sherry

➢  2/3 cup beef broth

➢  2/3 cup milk, dairy or vegan

➢  1 teaspoon freshly ground black pepper

➢  1/2 cup hulled barley

➢  1 pound beef tenderloin or tips

➢  12 ounces mushrooms, finely sliced

➢  4 cups butternut or acorn squashes, cubed

➢  4 cups frozen broccoli florets

*How to Prepare:*

1. Set the oven to 450 degrees Fahrenheit. Coat the inside of an oven-proof baking dish with nonstick cooking spray.

2. Arrange the onion in the dish. Add the barley on top.

3. In a bowl, combine the broth, milk, pepper, and sherry. Po half of the mixture into the baking dish, then stir.

4. Place the beef on top, followed by the mushrooms. Add t remaining broth mixture on top.

5. Place the squash on top of the beef, then add the broccoli.

Cover the baking dish and bake for 45 minutes, or until beef is cooked through. Serve at once.

## Easy Beef Chili

Number of Servings: 8

*What You'll Need:*

- ➤ 2 1/2 tablespoons coconut oil
- ➤ 3 onions, chopped
- ➤ 4 garlic cloves, minced
- ➤ 1 1/2 pounds lean ground beef
- ➤ 1 pound beef sirloin, cubed
- ➤ 3 cups tomatoes, diced
- ➤ 1 1/2 cup brewed coffee
- ➤ 1 1/2 cups tomato paste
- ➤ 3 cups beef broth
- ➤ 1 1/2 tablespoons unsweetened cocoa powder
- ➤ 1 1/2 tablespoons cumin seeds
- ➤ 1 1/2 teaspoons dried oregano
- ➤ 1 1/2 teaspoons ground coriander
- ➤ 1 1/2 teaspoons ground cayenne pepper
- ➤ 1 1/2 teaspoons sea salt
- ➤ 8 cups kidney beans, cooked
- ➤ 6 fresh hot chili peppers, chopped

*How to Prepare:*

Place a large pan over medium flame and heat the oil. Stir in the sirloin, ground beef, onion, and garlic. Cook until meat is browned.

Drain the grease, then stir in the tomatoes, coffee, tomato paste, broth, cocoa powder, cumin, oregano, coriander, cayenne, salt, kidney beans, and hot chili peppers.

Bring to a boil, then reduce to the lowest possible setting. Let simmer, partially covered, for 2 hours. Serve warm.

## Baked Steak Feast

Number of Servings: 4

*What You'll Need:*

- ➢ 2 cups beef or vegetable broth
- ➢ 2 cups uncooked brown rice, rinsed
- ➢ Juice from 4 limes
- ➢ 2 tablespoons fresh cilantro, chopped
- ➢ 2 tablespoons fresh oregano, chopped
- ➢ 2 teaspoons ground cumin
- ➢ 1 pound boneless beefsteak
- ➢ 8 garlic cloves, minced
- ➢ 1 onion, sliced thinly
- ➢ 1 yellow bell pepper, seeded and sliced
- ➢ 1 red bell pepper, seeded and sliced
- ➢ 1 green bell pepper, seeded and sliced
- ➢ Sea salt
- ➢ Freshly ground black pepper

*How to Prepare:*

1. Set the oven to 450 degrees Fahrenheit to preheat. Coat an 8 inch casserole dish with nonstick cooking spray.

In a bowl, combine the cilantro, cumin, oregano, and lime juice.

Season the steak with salt and pepper.

Combine the rice and broth in the prepared dish. Place the steak on top, then pour half of the herb mixture over the steak.

Sprinkle the garlic over the dish, then the bell peppers. Pour the remaining herb mixture all over.

Cover the casserole and bake for 1 hour, or until steak is cooked through. Turn off the heat and let stand for 5 minutes in the oven. Serve warm.

**Easy Goulash**

Number of Servings: 8

*What You'll Need:*

- ➢ 5 cups cauliflower florets

- ➢ 1 1/2 pounds ground beef

- ➢ 1 large onion, chopped

- ➢ 3 cups kidney beans, cooked

- ➢ 1 1/2 cups tomato paste

- ➢ Sea salt

- ➢ Freshly ground black pepper

- ➢ Garlic powder

*How to Prepare:*

1. Place a pan over medium heat and cook the ground beef until browned. Drain the excess grease, then stir in the garlic powder, salt, and pepper.

2. Add the kidney beans, cauliflowers, and tomato paste. Cover and cook over medium flame for 10 minutes, or until cauliflowers are tender. Serve warm.

## Stewed Cabbage and Beef

Number of Servings: 6

*What You'll Need:*

- 1 pound lean ground beef

- 3/4 cup beef broth

- 1 onion, chopped

- 1 bay leaf

- 1/3 teaspoon freshly ground black pepper

- 2 celery ribs, chopped

- 3 cups cabbage, finely grated

- 1 carrot, diced

- 1 cup tomato paste

- 1/4 teaspoon sea salt

*How to Prepare:*

Place a pan over medium-high flame and cook the ground beef until browned. Drain the excess fat.

Stir in the cabbage, carrot, beef broth, onion, bay leaf, celery, and pepper.

Cover and let simmer over low heat for 10 minutes, or until cabbage is wilted.

Stir in the tomato paste and let simmer, uncovered, for 15 minutes. Serve at once.

## Stifado

Number of Servings: 6

*What You'll Need:*

- ➢ 2 pounds beef osso bucco
- ➢ 15 whole shallots, peeled
- ➢ 2 bay leaves
- ➢ 6 garlic cloves
- ➢ 2 sprigs fresh rosemary
- ➢ 4 whole pimientos
- ➢ 3 whole cloves
- ➢ 1/3 teaspoon ground nutmeg
- ➢ 1/3 cup olive oil
- ➢ 1/4 cup apple cider vinegar
- ➢ 3/4 teaspoon sea salt
- ➢ 1/6 teaspoon freshly ground black pepper
- ➢ 1 1/2 cups tomato paste

*How to Prepare:*

1. Combine the olive oil, vinegar, and tomato paste in a bowl.
2. Combine the beef, shallots, garlic, bay leaves, rosema, pimientos, whole cloves, nutmeg, salt, and pepper in a larg pot.

Pour the olive oil mixture into the pot, then place over medium-high heat. Bring to a boil, then reduce heat to a simmer.

Let simmer for 2 hours on low (make sure it's covered). Shake the pot occasionally. Serve warm.

# Chapter 6: Pork Recipes

## Pork and Cabbage

Number of Servings: 3

*What You'll Need:*

- ➢ 1 1/2 pounds pork, sliced
- ➢ 2 small cabbages, finely grated
- ➢ 3 tablespoons tomato paste
- ➢ 3 cups tomatoes, chopped
- ➢ 3 tablespoons olive oil
- ➢ 1 1/2 tablespoons white wine vinegar
- ➢ 1 1/2 cups water
- ➢ 1 1/2 tablespoons fresh dill, chopped
- ➢ Sea salt
- ➢ Black pepper

*How to Prepare:*

1. Set the oven to 400 degrees Fahrenheit to preheat.
2. In an oven-safe pot, combine the tomato paste, dill, white wine vinegar, water, and olive oil. Mix well.
3. Add the pork tenderloin and turn to coat. Season with salt and pepper. Stir in the cabbage.

▲ Place the pot in the oven and cook for 50 minutes, or until pork is cooked through. Carefully take out of the oven and serve at once.

## Easy Pork Chops

Number of Servings: 6

*What You'll Need:*

- ➢ 6 pork loin chops
- ➢ 2 cups cream of mushroom soup
- ➢ 1 1/2 sleeves onion soup mix
- ➢ 2 1/4 cups long grain rice
- ➢ 3 1/2 cups water
- ➢ 1 1/2 cups frozen peas
- ➢ 2 cups broccoli florets
- ➢ 3/4 teaspoon garlic powder
- ➢ 3/4 teaspoon paprika

*How to Prepare:*

1. Pat the pork chops dry and season with garlic powder and paprika on both sides.

2. Set the oven to 350 degrees Fahrenheit to preheat. Coat a 10 4 inch baking pan with nonstick cooking spray.

3. In a bowl, combine the rice, water, mushrooms, and onion soup. Transfer to the prepared baking dish.

4. Pour the peas and broccoli into the dish, then place the pork chops on top.

Bake for 60 minutes (make sure it's covered) or until the pork chops are cooked through.

Remove the cover and bake for an additional 15 minutes, then serve.

## Pork and Kale Casserole

Number of Servings: 6

*What You'll Need:*

- ➢ 1 1/2 tablespoons coconut oil
- ➢ 1 1/2 pounds pork tenderloin, trimmed and chopped
- ➢ 1 teaspoon sea salt
- ➢ 1 large onion, minced
- ➢ 6 garlic cloves, minced
- ➢ 3 teaspoons paprika
- ➢ 1/3 teaspoon crushed red pepper
- ➢ 1 1/2 cups white wine
- ➢ 6 plum tomatoes, chopped
- ➢ 6 cups chicken or vegetable broth
- ➢ 2 bunches kale, chopped
- ➢ 3 cups white beans, cooked

*How to Prepare:*

1. Place a large pot over medium heat and add the oil. Stir in pork and onions and cook until pork is browned.

2. Stir in the the crushed red pepper, garlic, and paprika. Add wine, broth, tomatoes, beans ,and kale.

3. Bring to a boil, and then reduce to a simmer. Cook, partially covered, until kale is wilted. Serve at once.

# Pork Chop and Sauerkraut Casserole

Number of Servings: 8

*What You'll Need:*

- 12 slices bacon

- 35 ounces sauerkraut

- 8 pork chops (1/2-inch thick each)

- 6 russet potatoes, cubed

- 3 medium-sized onions, sliced

- 21 ounces canned tomatoes, stewed

- Sea salt

- Freshly ground black pepper

*How to Prepare:*

Set the oven to 350 degrees Fahrenheit to preheat. Lightly grease a 10 x 14 inch baking pan with nonstick cooking spray.

Season the pork chops with salt and pepper.

Arrange the bacon slices on the bottom, then spoon the sauerkraut on top. Place the pork chops over the sauerkraut, followed by the potato cubes, sliced onions, and finally the tomatoes.

Cover and bake for 2 hours, or until pork chops are cooked through. Serve warm.

## Pork and Green Beans

Number of Servings: 3

*What You'll Need:*

- ➤ 3 cups green beans (fresh or frozen), halved
- ➤ 2 onions, minced
- ➤ 3 garlic cloves, minced
- ➤ 1-inch fresh ginger root, peeled and crushed
- ➤ 3/4 teaspoon red pepper flakes
- ➤ 2 tomatoes, chopped
- ➤ 1 1/2 tablespoons coconut oil
- ➤ 3/4 cup chicken broth
- ➤ 1 1/2 pounds lean pork tenderloin, chopped
- ➤ 1/2 lemon, sliced into wedges
- ➤ Sea salt
- ➤ Freshly ground black pepper

*How to Prepare:*

1. Place a pot over medium flame and heat the oil. Add the onions, garlic, ginger, and pork. Cook until pork is browned.

2. Stir in the broth, tomatoes, green beans, and red pepper. Let simmer while covered for 10 minutes or until green beans are fork-tender.

Season with salt and pepper to taste, then serve with lemon wedges.

## Spiced Pork with Honey Glaze

Number of Servings: 4

*What You'll Need:*

- ➤ 1 pound pork tenderloin
- ➤ 1/2 cup honey
- ➤ 1/4 cup Dijon mustard
- ➤ 1 teaspoon ground cinnamon
- ➤ 1 teaspoon ground ginger
- ➤ 1/2 teaspoon ground cloves
- ➤ 12 small potatoes, halved
- ➤ 4 carrots, sliced into coins
- ➤ 4 cups green beans (frozen or fresh), cut
- ➤ Sea salt
- ➤ Freshly ground black pepper

*How to Prepare:*

1. Set the oven to 450 degrees Fahrenheit to preheat. Coat an 8 x 8 inch baking dish with nonstick cooking spray.

2. Season the pork tenderloin with salt and pepper. Place the pork inside the baking dish.

3. Combine the mustard, honey, cloves, ginger, and cinnamon in a bowl, then pour on top of the pork.

Arrange the carrots, green beans, and potatoes around the pork.

Cover the dish and bake for 50 minutes, then turn off the heat and let stand in the oven for 5 minutes. Serve warm.

## Pinto Beans and Pork Dinner

Number of Servings: 8

*What You'll Need:*

- ➢ 1 1/2 pounds pinto beans, cooked
- ➢ 7 garlic cloves, chopped
- ➢ 1 1/2 teaspoons sea salt
- ➢ 1 pound boneless pork, diced
- ➢ 2 onions, chopped
- ➢ 4 large tomatoes, diced
- ➢ 2 jalapeño peppers, sliced
- ➢ 1/2 cup fresh cilantro, chopped

*How to Prepare:*

1. Place a large pan over high heat and cook the pork until browned. Drain the excess grease. Stir in the onion, jalapeño and tomatoes and cook until tender.

2. Put the mixture into a slow cooker, then stir in the pinto beans. Cover and cook for 4 hours on low heat.

3. Before serving, stir in the cilantro.

# Stewed Pork and Sweet Potato

Number of Servings: 6

*What You'll Need:*

1 cup tomato paste

2 1/2 tablespoons lemon juice

1 1/2 tablespoons Dijon mustard

1/3 teaspoon sea salt

1/6 teaspoon freshly ground black pepper

2 tablespoons chunky almond butter

2 sweet potatoes, peeled and cubed

1/3 teaspoon garlic, minced

3 pounds boneless pork loin

*How to Prepare:*

Combine the almond butter, tomato paste, mustard, and lemon juice in a bowl. Add the garlic, pepper, salt, and sweet potato.

Put the pork loin in the slow cooker and pour the paste over it. Turn to coat.

Cover and cook for 8 hours on low. Serve warm.

## Quinoa and Sausage Pot

Number of Servings: 4

*What You'll Need:*

- ➤ 1 1/2 cups quinoa, rinsed thoroughly
- ➤ 2 cups chicken or vegetable broth
- ➤ 1 pound pork sausage links
- ➤ 1 yellow bell pepper, seeded and sliced
- ➤ 1 green bell pepper, seeded and sliced
- ➤ 1 red bell pepper, seeded and sliced
- ➤ 8 plum tomatoes, quartered
- ➤ Sea salt

*How to Prepare:*

1. Set the oven to 450 degrees Fahrenheit to preheat. Coat an 8 inch baking dish with nonstick cooking spray.

2. Combine the quinoa and broth in the baking dish, then a the sausages on top, followed by the bell peppers.

3. Season everything with salt, then arrange the quarter tomatoes on top.

4. Cover the baking dish. Bake for 45 minutes or until pork cooked through. Turn off the heat and let the dish stand in t oven for 5 minutes.

5. Fluff up the quinoa using a fork, then serve.

# Chapter 7: Poultry and Seafood Recipes

## Cheesy Chicken Casserole
Number of Servings: 6

*What You'll Need:*

6 cups skinless and boneless chicken meat, cubed

3 cups croutons

3 cups Swiss cheese

1 2/3 cups of your favorite salad dressing

3/4 cup low-fat milk

3 cups frozen corn

6 celery stalks, rinsed and thinly sliced

*How to Prepare:*

Coat a skillet with nonstick cooking spray and place over medium heat. Cook the cubed chicken until golden brown, then transfer to a large bowl.

Set the oven to 350 degrees Fahrenheit to preheat.

Add the croutons, cheese, salad dressing, milk, corn, and celery into the bowl and mix everything well.

Transfer the mixture into a 10 x 4 inch baking dish (approximately 4 quarts).

Bake for 40 minutes, then serve.

## Chicken Paella

Number of Servings: 3

*What You'll Need:*

- ➤ 3 cups skinless and boneless chicken breast, diced
- ➤ 3 cups brown or white rice, uncooked
- ➤ 1 1/2 cups canned green peas, drained
- ➤ 6 cups vegetable broth
- ➤ 1 white onion, diced
- ➤ Sea salt
- ➤ Freshly ground black pepper
- ➤ Saffron
- ➤ Olive oil

*How to Prepare:*

1. Place a nonstick skillet over medium heat and lightly grea_ with olive oil. Cook the chicken breast until browned, th remove from heat and set aside.

2. Set the oven to 400 degrees Fahrenheit to preheat.

3. In an oven-safe pot, combine the cooked chicken with tn green peas and onion. Add the rice and broth, then a da each of salt, pepper, and saffron.

4. Place the pot in the oven (make sure it's covered) and cook i. 60 minutes. Carefully take out of the oven and serve at once.

# Chicken Noodle Casserole

Number of Servings: 6

*What You'll Need:*

6 skinless and boneless chicken breasts, cubed

20 ounces egg noodles, cooked

3 cups sour cream

1 1/4 cups mozzarella cheese, finely grated

1 1/4 cups cheddar cheese, finely grated

38 ounces canned cream of mushroom soup

1 1/2 cups crackers, crushed

1/3 cup butter or margarine, melted

*How to Prepare:*

Coat a skillet with nonstick cooking spray and place over medium heat. Cook the cubed chicken until golden brown, then transfer to a large bowl.

Set the oven to 350 degrees Fahrenheit. Coat a 10 x 4 inch baking dish (approximately 4 quarts) with nonstick cooking spray.

Add the soup, sour cream, and cheese. Mix well. Stir in the cooked egg noodles, then transfer to the the prepared baking dish.

In a bowl, combine the melted butter or margarine with the crushed crackers, then spread evenly over the chicken mixture.

5.  Bake for 30 to 40 minutes or till cheese is melted and top golden brown.

# Honey and Sesame Chicken and Quinoa

Number of Servings: 5

*What You'll Need:*

- 2 pounds chicken breast, diced
- 2 cups broccoli florets
- 1 cup uncooked quinoa, rinsed thoroughly
- 2 small onions, diced
- 4 garlic cloves, sliced
- 1 cup honey
- 1 cup water
- 2 tablespoons sesame seeds
- Sea salt
- Freshly ground black pepper

*How to Prepare:*

Set the oven to 400 degrees Fahrenheit to preheat.

In an oven-safe pot, combine the chicken, broccoli, quinoa, water, onion, garlic, honey, and sesame seeds. Season with salt and pepper.

Place the pot in the oven (make sure it's covered) and cook for 45 minutes. Carefully take out of the oven and serve at once.

## Parsnip and Turkey Dish

Number of Servings: 3

*What You'll Need:*

- ➢ 1 1/2 pounds turkey breast, chopped
- ➢ 1 1/2 cups parsnips, sliced
- ➢ 3 cups tomato sauce
- ➢ 1 1/2 cups celery, finely sliced
- ➢ 2 small onions, sliced
- ➢ 3 tablespoons olive oil
- ➢ 3/4 teaspoon dried thyme
- ➢ 1/2 cups fresh flat leaf parsley, chopped
- ➢ Sea salt
- ➢ Freshly ground black pepper

*How to Prepare:*

1. Set the oven to 400 degrees Fahrenheit to preheat.

2. In an oven-safe pot, combine the tomato sauce, onion, olive oil, celery, thyme, parsley, parsnips, and turkey breast. Season with salt and pepper.

3. Place the pot in the oven and cook for 90 minutes, or until the turkey is cooked through. Carefully take out of the oven and serve at once.

# Sweet Corn and Tuna

Number of Servings: 5

*What You'll Need:*

- 4 cups canned tuna chunks, drained

- 1 1/2 canned green beans, drained

- 1 1/2 canned sweet corn, drained

- 1 large red onion, sliced

- 1 1/2 cups red peppers, sliced

- 1 1/2 tablespoons olive oil

- 1 1/2 cups water

- Sea salt

- Freshly ground black pepper

*How to Prepare:*

Set the oven to 400 degrees Fahrenheit to preheat.

In an oven-safe pot, combine the water, green beans, sweet corn, red onion, red peppers, and tuna chunks. Drizzle olive oil on top and season with salt and pepper.

Place the pot in the oven and cook for 45 minutes. Carefully take out of the oven and serve at once.

## Mussels and Quinoa Casserole

Number of Servings: 4

*What You'll Need:*

➤ 3 cups quinoa

➤ 4 1/2 cups water

➤ 3 cups mussels, rinsed and drained

➤ 2 small onions, sliced

➤ 2 cups baby spinach

➤ 3 garlic cloves, sliced

➤ Sea salt

➤ Freshly ground black pepper

*How to Prepare:*

1. Set the oven to 400 degrees Fahrenheit to preheat.

2. In an oven-safe pot, combine the quinoa and water. Stir in t. mussels, onion, baby spinach, and garlic. Season with salt a pepper.

3. Place the pot in the oven and cook for 45 minutes, or until t quinoa is fluffy and the mussels have opened. Carefully ta out of the oven and discard any unopened mussels. Serve a once.

# Salmon and Peas in Rice

Number of Servings: 6

*What You'll Need:*

6 salmon fillets

3 cups white rice, uncooked

6 cups vegetable broth

1 1/2 cups canned peas, drained

2 small red onions, diced

Zest of 1 1/2 lemons

1 1/2 tablespoons fresh parsley, chopped

Sea salt

Freshly ground black pepper

*How to Prepare:*

Set the oven to 400 degrees Fahrenheit to preheat.

In an oven-safe pot, combine the rice and broth. Stir in the peas, onion, and salmon fillets.

Add the zest and parsley, then season with salt and pepper.

Place the pot in the oven and cook (make sure it's covered) for 50 minutes or until fish is cooked through and rice is fluffy. Carefully take out of the oven and serve at once.

# Eggplant and Shrimp Casserole

Number of Servings: 4

*What You'll Need:*

- ➤ 20 shrimps, peeled and deveined
- ➤ 1 large eggplant, sliced
- ➤ 3 cups tomato sauce
- ➤ 2 small onions, sliced
- ➤ 1 1/2 tablespoons olive oil
- ➤ 3 teaspoons lemon juice
- ➤ 3/4 teaspoon chili pepper flakes
- ➤ Sea salt
- ➤ Freshly ground black pepper

*How to Prepare:*

1. Set the oven to 400 degrees Fahrenheit to preheat.

2. In an oven-safe pot, combine the shrimp, eggplant, tomato sauce, onion, olive oil, and lemon juice. Season with chili pepper flakes, salt, and pepper.

3. Place the pot in the oven and cook for 15 minutes, or until the shrimp is pink and cooked through. Carefully take out of oven and serve at once.

## Mackerel in Tomato Sauce

Number of Servings: 6

*What You'll Need:*

6 mackerels, washed and chopped

3 cups tomatoes, chopped

2 tablespoons tomato paste

2 cups water

6 garlic cloves, chopped

2 tablespoons fresh parsley, chopped

2 teaspoon sweet red paprika

Sea salt

Freshly ground black pepper

*How to Prepare:*

Set the oven to 400 degrees Fahrenheit to preheat.

In an oven-safe pot, combine the tomato paste and water. Stir in the tomatoes, garlic, parsley, and sweet red paprika.

Place the mackerel slices over the sauce and turn to coat. Season with salt and pepper.

Place the pot in the oven and cook for 50 minutes, or until fish is cooked through. Carefully take out of the oven and serve at once.

# Chapter 8: Dump Cake Recipes

## Pineapple and Cherry Dump Cake

Number of Servings: 8

*What You'll Need:*

- ➢ 20 ounces canned pineapple, crushed

- ➢ 28 ounces canned cherry pie filling

- ➢ 24 ounces yellow or white cake mix

- ➢ 1 1/2 cups walnuts, chopped

- ➢ 1 cup butter, melted

*How to Prepare:*

1. Set the oven to 350 degrees Fahrenheit to preheat. Coat a 10 4 inch baking pan with nonstick cooking spray.

2. Fill the bottom of the pan with the cherry pie mix, then add the crushed pineapple on top evenly.

3. Carefully pour the cake mix on top of the pineapple evenly well, then top with the chopped walnuts.

4. Moisten everything with the melted butter, then bake for minutes or until golden brown. Poke the center with toothpick, and if it comes out clean, take the cake out of the oven.

5. Set on a wire rack to cool before slicing. Serve chilled or room temperature, preferably with whipped cream or cream.

# Pumpkin Harvest Dump Cake

Number of Servings: 12

*What You'll Need:*

- 38 ounces pumpkin pie mix
- 3/4 cup brown sugar
- 1 1/4 tablespoons pumpkin pie spice
- 24 ounces yellow or white cake mix
- 1 cup walnuts, chopped
- 1 cup butter, melted

*How to Prepare:*

1. Set the oven to 350 degrees Fahrenheit to preheat. Coat a 10 x 4 inch baking pan with nonstick cooking spray.

2. Fill the bottom of the pan with the pumpkin pie mix, then carefully pour the cake mix on top evenly.

3. Top with the chopped walnuts, then moisten everything with the melted butter.

4. Bake for 50 minutes or until golden brown. Poke the center with a toothpick, and if it comes out clean, take the cake out of the oven.

5. Set on a wire rack to cool before slicing. Serve chilled or at room temperature, preferably with whipped cream or ice cream.

## Plum Dump Cake

Number of Servings: 8

*What You'll Need:*

- ➤ 20 ounces canned plums with syrup
- ➤ 14 ounces plum preserves
- ➤ 24 ounces yellow cake mix
- ➤ 2/3 cup pecans, crushed
- ➤ 1/3 teaspoon cinnamon
- ➤ 1 cup butter, melted

*How to Prepare:*

1. Set the oven to 350 degrees Fahrenheit to preheat. Coat a 10 × 4 inch baking pan with nonstick cooking spray.

2. Fill the bottom of the pan with the canned plums with syrup, then add the plum preserves on top evenly.

3. Carefully pour the cake mix on top of the plum preserves evenly as well, then top with the crushed pecans and cinnamon.

4. Moisten everything with the melted butter, then bake for 45 minutes or until golden brown. Poke the center with a toothpick, and if it comes out clean, take the cake out of the oven.

5. Set on a wire rack to cool before slicing. Serve chilled or room temperature, preferably with whipped cream or ice cream.

## eberry Lemon Dump Cake

Number of Servings: 10

*What You'll Need:*

25 ounces blueberry pie filling

20 ounces canned pineapple, crushed

24 ounces yellow lemon cake mix

1 cup butter, melted

*How to Prepare:*

Set the oven to 350 degrees Fahrenheit to preheat. Coat a 10 x 4 inch baking pan with nonstick cooking spray.

Fill the bottom of the pan with the blueberry pie filling, then add the crushed pineapple on top evenly.

Carefully pour the cake mix on top of the pineapple evenly as well, then moisten everything with the melted butter.

Bake for 45 minutes or until golden brown. Poke the center with a toothpick, and if it comes out clean, take the cake out of the oven.

Set on a wire rack to cool before slicing. Serve chilled or at room temperature, preferably with whipped cream or ice cream.

## Peach Dump Cake

Number of Servings: 8

*What You'll Need:*

➢ 40 ounces canned peaches in syrup, sliced

➢ 24 ounces yellow or white cake mix

➢ 1 cup pecans, chopped

➢ 1 cup butter, melted

*How to Prepare:*

1. Set the oven to 350 degrees Fahrenheit to preheat. Coat a 10 4 inch baking pan with nonstick cooking spray.

2. Fill the bottom of the pan with the sliced peaches and the syrup, then carefully pour the cake mix on top evenly.

3. Top with the chopped walnuts, then moisten everything with the melted butter.

4. Bake for 40 minutes or until golden brown. Poke the center with a toothpick, and if it comes out clean, take the cake out of the oven.

5. Set on a wire rack to cool before slicing. Serve chilled or room temperature, preferably with whipped cream or ice cream.

# Strawberry Dump Cake

Number of Servings: 8

*What You'll Need:*

- 1 1/4 pounds fresh strawberries, hulled and sliced (or 25 ounces strawberry pie filling)

- 24 ounces white cake mix

- 1 cup butter, melted

*How to Prepare:*

Set the oven to 350 degrees Fahrenheit to preheat. Coat a 10 x 4 inch baking pan with nonstick cooking spray.

Fill the bottom of the pan with the strawberries or strawberry pie filling, then carefully pour the cake mix on top evenly.

Moisten everything with the melted butter, then bake for 40 minutes or until golden brown. Poke the center with a toothpick, and if it comes out clean, take the cake out of the oven.

Set on a wire rack to cool before slicing. Serve chilled or at room temperature, preferably with whipped cream or ice cream.

## Apple and Apricot Dump Cake

Number of Servings: 8

*What You'll Need:*

- ➢ 26 ounces canned apple pie filling

- ➢ 20 ounces canned apricots in syrup, sliced

- ➢ 24 ounces yellow or white cake mix

- ➢ 1 cup walnuts, chopped

- ➢ 1 cup butter, melted

*How to Prepare:*

1. Set the oven to 350 degrees Fahrenheit to preheat. Coat a 1(
   4 inch baking pan with nonstick cooking spray.

2. Fill the bottom of the pan with the cherry pie filling, then a
   the sliced apricots on top evenly. Drizzle a bit of the apric
   syrup all over.

3. Carefully pour the cake mix on top of the apricots evenly, th
   top with the chopped walnuts.

4. Moisten everything with the melted butter, then bake for
   minutes or until golden brown. Poke the center with
   toothpick, and if it comes out clean, take the cake out of th
   oven.

5. Set on a wire rack to cool before slicing. Serve chilled or a
   room temperature, preferably with whipped cream or i
   cream.

# White Chocolate and Raspberry Dump Cake

Number of Servings: 8

*What You'll Need:*

- 25 ounces canned raspberry pie filling
- 10 ounces canned pineapple with juice, crushed
- 24 ounces yellow or white cake mix
- 1 1/4 cups white chocolate chips or buttons
- 1 cup butter, melted

*How to Prepare:*

Set the oven to 350 degrees Fahrenheit to preheat. Coat a 10 x 4 inch baking pan with nonstick cooking spray.

Fill the bottom of the pan with the raspberry pie mix, then add the crushed pineapple with the juice on top evenly.

Carefully pour the cake mix on top of the pineapple evenly as well, then add the white chocolate chips or buttons on top.

Moisten everything with the melted butter, then bake for 40 minutes or until golden brown. Poke the center with a toothpick, and if it comes out clean, take the cake out of the oven.

Set on a wire rack to cool before slicing. Serve chilled or at room temperature, preferably with whipped cream or ice cream.

## Chocolate and Cherry Dump Cake

Number of Servings: 8

*What You'll Need:*

➤ 25 ounces canned cherry pie filling

➤ 1 1/4 cups semi-sweet or dark chocolate chips

➤ 24 ounces yellow or white cake mix

➤ 1 cup butter, melted

*How to Prepare:*

1. Set the oven to 325 degrees Fahrenheit to preheat. Coat a 10 x 4 inch baking pan with nonstick cooking spray.

2. Fill the bottom of the pan with the cherry pie mix, then add the chocolate chips on top evenly.

3. Carefully pour the cake mix on top of the chocolate chips evenly as well, then moisten everything with the melted butter.

4. Bake for 40 minutes or until golden brown. Poke the center with a toothpick, and if it comes out clean, take the cake out of the oven.

5. Set on a wire rack to cool before slicing. Serve chilled or at room temperature, preferably with whipped cream or ice cream.

# Pineapple and Orange Dump Cake

Number of Servings: 10

*What You'll Need:*

- 10 ounces orange preserves

- 15 ounces canned pineapple with juice

- 24 ounces white or orange cake mix

- 1 1/4 cups coconut, finely grated

- 1 cup butter, melted

*How to Prepare:*

Set the oven to 350 degrees Fahrenheit to preheat. Coat a 10 x 4 inch baking pan with nonstick cooking spray.

Fill the bottom of the pan with the orange preserves, then add the pineapple with the juices on top evenly.

Carefully pour the cake mix on top of the pineapple evenly as well, then top with the finely grated coconut.

Moisten everything with the melted butter, then bake for 40 minutes or until golden brown. Poke the center with a toothpick, and if it comes out clean, take the cake out of the oven.

Set on a wire rack to cool before slicing. Serve chilled or at room temperature, preferably with whipped cream or ice cream.

# Conclusion

I hope this book was able to help you to prepare dump dinner easily at home, and inspire you to create your own dump dinner recipes during your spare time.

The next step is to prepare a grocery list and weekly meal plan that will enable you to make full use of these recipes. Have experimenting in the kitchen!

I wish you the best of luck!

*John Web*